Our Democracy

Ariella Tievsky

Contents

The People's Choice

It's election day. People are lined up to vote for our country's president. This scene takes place every four years in the United States. That's because our country is a **democracy.** Many other countries around the world are democracies, too.

In a democracy, people vote to choose their leaders. The leaders have to prove they can do a good job if they want to get elected!

America wasn't always a democracy. The first settlers who came here from Europe were ruled by the king of England. No one elected the kings and queens of England. They ruled because their father, or someone else in their family, ruled before them. What happened if the king or queen didn't do a good job? Kings and queens usually ruled until they died. Then one of their children or other relatives took over.

The last king of England to rule America was George III. England still has kings and queens today, but the government is run as a democracy.

No More Kings!

Americans got tired of being ruled by England. In 1776, they sent the king their **Declaration of Independence.** This was a list of complaints about the way the king and his **government** had treated them. Americans told the king that from now on they would be independent, or free. They would govern themselves.

The king was not happy! He sent soldiers to keep the Americans under English rule. That was the beginning of the **American Revolution.** As you know, the Americans fought back and won their independence.

Paul Revere warned people that the English soldiers were coming to attack. His warning gave the Americans time to prepare for battle.

Democracy Is Different

Americans didn't want their country to be ruled by a king or queen. Their leaders created a plan for a new kind of government. Today, we still use that plan. It's called the **Constitution.** It says that the United States is a democracy.

In a democracy, we elect our leaders. We have a president instead of a king or queen, but the president doesn't have complete power. No one person does!

Some people thought that George Washington should be king. Instead, Washington became the first president of the United States in 1789.

The Constitution of the United States

Who Does What in Our Democracy?

The people who wrote the Constitution didn't want one person or group to have too much power. They made sure this wouldn't happen by dividing the government into three separate parts, or branches. Each branch had a separate job, and the branches had the power to check up on each other. This is how our government still works.

United States Capitol Building, Washington, D.C.

The Three Branches of Government

Legislative Branch
Makes laws

Judicial Branch
Makes decisions about laws

Executive Branch
Makes sure laws are followed

Our Lawmakers

The **legislative branch** of our government, or **Congress,** makes our laws. Even Congress is divided into parts. These parts are called the **Senate** and the **House of Representatives.**

People in each state elect the senators and representatives they will send to Congress. Each state has two senators. The House of Representatives is different. States with more people have more representatives in Congress.

Georgia Representative John Lewis

Georgia Representative Jack Kingston

Our Judges

The most important people in the **judicial branch** are judges. Judges in some courts decide how to punish people who have broken the law. Sometimes people disagree about the meaning of a law. If this happens, judges settle arguments about what the law really means.

The **Supreme Court** is the highest court in the United States. Its nine judges decide if decisions made by lower courts are right. They also decide if laws made by Congress follow the Constitution. This is how the judicial branch checks up on the legislative branch.

This is the main room of the United States Supreme Court. The nine judges, or justices, sit in the chairs in the front of the room. Visitors are allowed inside when the court meets.

Sandra Day O'Connor was the first woman to become a Supreme Court Justice.

Thurgood Marshall was the first African American to become a Supreme Court Justice.

Our President

The **executive branch** of our government is in charge of making sure that people obey the country's laws. Our president is the head of the executive branch. The people vote for a president and vice president every four years. Here are just a few of the president's most important jobs:

- Be commander-in-chief of the armed forces
- Give Congress a plan on how to spend the country's money
- Suggest laws to Congress
- Meet with the leaders of other countries

Franklin D. Roosevelt was president from 1933 to 1945. He led the country to victory in a major war, called World War II.

Many people help the president. Here Ronald Reagan, who was president from 1981 to 1989, meets with other members of the executive branch.

State Governments

Your state has a government too, with its own constitution and its own leaders. State governments have three branches, just like the government of the whole country.

The leaders of Georgia's government meet in the state's capital city, Atlanta.

For example, Georgia's people elect representatives and senators to make laws. Judges work in Georgia's judicial branch. The people of the state elect the governor, who is the head of Georgia's executive branch.

A state government provides services, such as state parks for people to enjoy and state highways for cars and trucks to travel on.

Local Governments

You live in a country and a state. You also live in a community. Communities have governments too. The people elect community leaders, such as a mayor.

Local governments provide services for the community. Did you ride the bus to school today? Maybe you saw a fire truck or a police car rushing to help someone. These are examples of services that your local government may provide. The services are paid for with taxes —money people in the community pay to the government.

Mayor Shirley Franklin of Atlanta, Georgia

Our Leaders Work for Us

If Congress makes our laws, what do we the people have to say about them? A lot—because **citizens** choose the lawmakers by voting. A government that works this way is called a **representative democracy.** The people don't make laws or vote on laws, but they choose the lawmakers.

Today, all citizens who are 18 years and older can vote. This wasn't always true. When our country began, the only people who could vote were white men. Look at the time line on page 13 to see how this has changed.

In 1965, President Lyndon Johnson signed the Voting Rights Act. This law protected the voting rights of African Americans.

The Voice of the People

Americans have another very important right—freedom of speech. This means that people are allowed to say what they believe. We can agree or disagree with our government.

What happens if we disagree with our lawmakers? We can let them know what we think. And remember—our leaders have to pay attention to what voters say. They want all the votes they can get!

We can make our complaints heard by gathering for a protest.

We can write or sign a **petition.**

Voting Becomes More Fair

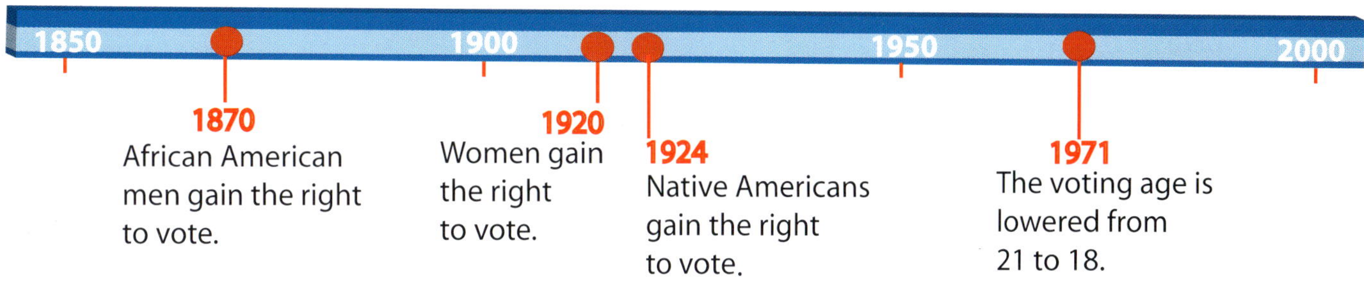

The People Speak

Many people have used their freedom of speech to make our democracy better. Some of them have become famous, and we remember them with pride.

**Frederick Douglass
about 1818–1895**

Frederick Douglass was born into slavery in Maryland. When he was 20 years old, he escaped. Douglass gave speeches that let people know what it was like to be a slave. He also wrote newspaper articles and books. He convinced many people that slavery was wrong and should be ended.

**Susan B. Anthony
1820–1906**

In 1872, Susan B. Anthony was arrested for voting! At that time, women were not allowed to vote. Anthony worked to organize meetings and protests for women's rights. Women finally gained the right to vote in 1920.

Mary McLeod Bethune
1875–1955

When Mary McLeod Bethune was a child, many people did not think African American children needed to get an education. So when she grew up, Bethune opened a school for African American girls. She spoke out and worked for equal rights for all African Americans.

Cesar Chavez
1927–1993

Cesar Chavez helped farmworkers, especially those who picked grapes. They worked long hours and were paid little. Chavez formed a group, or union, to get the farmworkers together. They got farm owners to treat them more fairly. The union Chavez started still protects farmworkers and their families today.

Democracy Long Ago

Americans weren't the first people to think of the idea of democracy. It began thousands of years ago, long before the first English settlers came here. To find out where democracy started, let's take a trip back in time to the city of Athens, in ancient Greece.

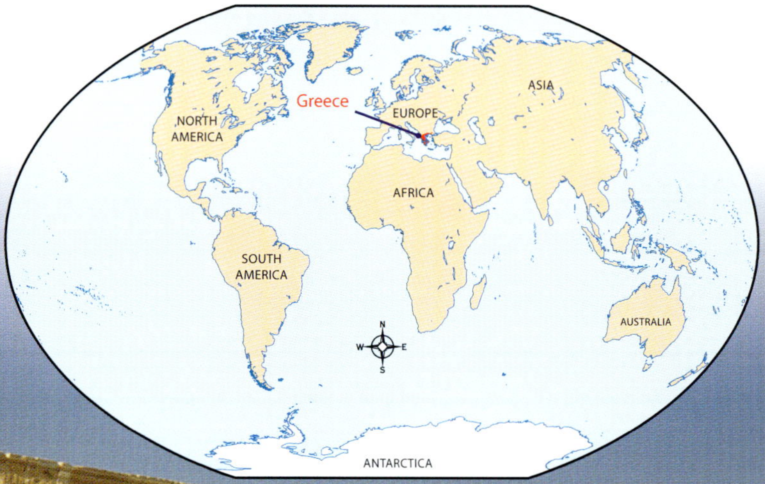

Greece
NORTH AMERICA
EUROPE
ASIA
AFRICA
SOUTH AMERICA
AUSTRALIA
ANTARCTICA
N
W
E
S

Ruins of the ancient Parthenon in Athens, Greece

Rule by the People

Today is a meeting day for the Assembly in ancient Athens. About 5,000 citizens climb to the top of a high hill to discuss their laws. They are all men. Women, slaves, and people who were not born in Athens cannot be citizens.

To start the meeting, a man called the herald yells out, "Who wishes to speak?" One citizen gets up to tell how he thinks spies should be punished. Others talk about different topics. Discussions aren't always quiet—sometimes fights break out between citizens who disagree!

The citizens of Athens don't have lawmakers as we do. They will vote on the laws themselves. That is why the government of ancient Athens is a **direct democracy,** and not a representative democracy, like ours.

In ancient Athens, every citizen had the right to speak in the Assembly.

Comparing Democracies

Our trip back in time has shown that we got some of our ideas about democracy from the ancient Greeks. In some ways though, our democracy is very different.

For example, all citizens of the United States over 18—men and women—are allowed to vote. Look at the chart to compare the two kinds of democracy.

Two Democracies

Compare	Athens Long Ago	United States Today
What type of democracy is it?	Direct democracy	Representative democracy
Who can vote?	Free adult men born in Athens	All citizens 18 or older
Who makes the laws?	Citizens	Elected representatives
How many people vote?	About 5,000	More than 100 million

From Greek to English

One clue that tells us where the idea of democracy began is in the word itself. "Democracy" comes from two Greek words, *demos*, which means "people," and *kratos* which means "rule." Put the two words together and you have the meaning of democracy—"rule by the people."

Which do you think is better—a direct democracy or a representative democracy? Can you think of any reasons that a representative democracy might work better in the United States?

Here's a hint. About 5,000 people voted in ancient Athens. More than 100 million people vote in the United States. Can you imagine having that many people discussing every law and then voting on it?

In the United States, citizens must sign up, or register, to vote in an election.

Gifts from Ancient Greece

Many important public buildings in the United States were built to look like buildings in ancient Greece. Look at the photographs on these pages to compare and contrast these buildings. How are they alike? How are they different?

The Parthenon
Athens, Greece

The Parthenon was built in ancient Athens more than 2,500 years ago. It was a temple built to honor Athena, the Greek goddess of wisdom. The Parthenon is made mostly of white marble.

The United States
Supreme Court Building
Washington, D.C.

The United States Supreme Court Building is in Washington, D.C. The designer wanted it to look important and remind people of ancient Greece, where democracy began.

Cities Called Athens

Why do you think so many cities and towns in the United States are called Athens?

The Lincoln Memorial
Washington, D.C.

The Lincoln Memorial is also in Washington, D.C. It was built to honor our sixteenth president, Abraham Lincoln. The memorial is made of marble from different parts of the United States.

Athens–Clarke County Courthouse
Athens, Georgia

Public buildings all over the United States were often built to look like ancient Greek buildings. How is this courthouse in Athens, Georgia, like the Parthenon?

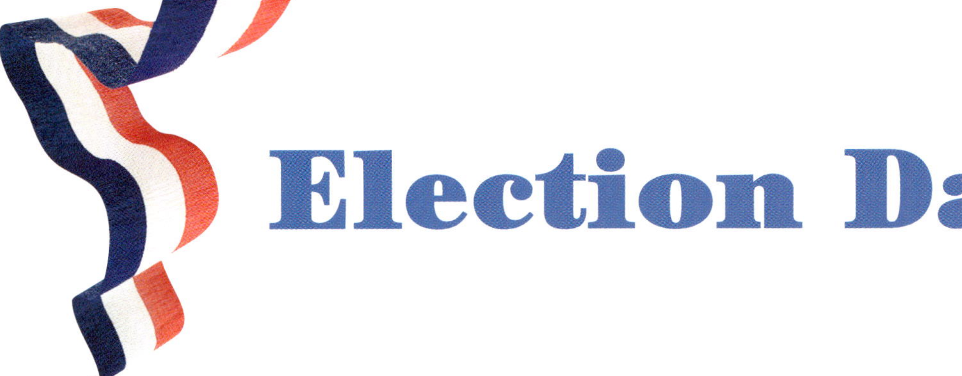

Election Day

Let's go back to where this book started—election day in the United States. Now that you've learned about democracy what do you think about these questions?

Why is it important for all Americans to vote?

When people vote, they choose leaders to make important decisions for all of us. For example, leaders decide about where to send our soldiers, or how to help businesses grow.

President George W. Bush and First Lady Laura Bush

How do people decide which person to vote for?

People read newspapers and listen to news broadcasts. They watch **candidates** speak on television. They think about what they read and hear.

How else can people take part in our country's democracy?

Keeping up with the news in the community is a first step. Telling leaders whether they are doing a good job is another. During an election, people might work to help one of the candidates.

You can take part in our democracy even if you're not old enough to vote yet.

Our government is always changing. Citizens elect new leaders. The leaders make new decisions and write new laws. One day you'll be able to vote for our country's leaders. Who knows? Maybe you'll even become a leader in our democracy!

Glossary

American Revolution the war fought by the Americans to gain their independence from England, from 1775 to 1783

candidate a person who runs for office

citizen a person who is a member of a country

Congress the part of the government that makes our laws

Constitution the written plan for our country's government

Declaration of Independence the statement written by Americans in 1776 saying that they were no longer part of England

democracy a system of government where the people elect their leaders

direct democracy a democracy where people make and vote on laws themselves

executive branch the branch of our government that makes sure people follow our country's laws

government people and laws that control a country, state, city, or town

House of Representatives one of the two parts of the United States Congress

judicial branch the branch of our government that makes decisions about laws

legislative branch the branch of our government that makes laws

petition a letter signed by many people stating their opinion about a particular issue

representative democracy a democracy where people elect leaders to represent them in government

Senate one of the two parts of the United States Congress

Supreme Court the highest court in the United States